The C

SCOOBY DOO 2™
MONSTERS UNLEASHED

Monster Joke Book

By Howie Dewin

PUFFIN

PUFFIN BOOKS

Published by the Penguin Group
Penguin Books Ltd, 80 Strand, London WC2R 0RL, England
Penguin Group (USA), Inc., 375 Hudson Street, New York, New York 10014, USA
Penguin Books Australia Ltd, 250 Camberwell Road, Camberwell,
Victoria 3124, Australia
Penguin Books Canada Ltd, 10 Alcorn Avenue, Toronto, Ontario, Canada M4V 3B2
Penguin Books India (P) Ltd, 11 Community Centre, Panchsheel Park,
New Delhi – 110 017, India
Penguin Books (NZ) Ltd, Cnr Rosedale and Airborne Roads, Albany, Auckland,
New Zealand
Penguin Books (South Africa) (Pty) Ltd, 24 Sturdee Avenue, Rosebank 2196,
South Africa

Penguin Books Ltd, Registered Offices: 80 Strand, London WC2R 0RL, England

www.penguin.com

First published in the USA by Scholastic Inc. 2004
First published in Great Britain in Puffin Books 2004

1

Copyright © 2004 by Hanna-Barbera.
SCOOBY-DOO and all related characters and elements are trademarks of and
© Hanna-Barbera.
(s04)

Cover design by Louise Bova
Interior design by Bethany Dixon

Set in Phoenix chunky 10/16pt and Coop forged 14/16pt

Made and printed in Clays Ltd, St Ives plc

British Library Cataloguing in Publication Data
A CIP catalogue record for this book is available from the British Library

ISBN 0–141–31812–0

Hey there, mystery fans!

Greetings from the Coolsonian Criminology Museum, the grooviest museum ever built. It's jam-packed with amazing stuff from Coolsville's hottest detectives' (that's us!) biggest cases. You'll see displays of the scariest costumes we've ever pulled off a bad guy (or girl).

But don't be afraid! Take the tour with us. We're so brave we can make jokes about anything. That's how it is when you're really, really cooooool. (But you probably know that.)

So keep your eye out for the Black Knight Ghost, the 10,000 Volt Ghost, Chickenstein, Skeleton Man, Redbeard's Ghost, the Creeper, the Ozark Witch and the Cotton Candy Glob.

Yikes! It's getting scary just talking about it. Time for some jokes!

Yours in yuks,

Over 200 Monsters Defeated

Scooby Shaggy Velma Daphne Fred

Scientific Name
Mysteromous Coolisis

Common Name
**Meet Coolsville's
Coolest Kids**

Fred here — the good-looking,
athletic, fearless brains behind
Mystery, Inc. Here are a few
groovy jokes for you!

Why are athletes so cool?
Because they're always
surrounded by fans!

What's a sprinter's favourite drink?
Running water.

**If athletes get athlete's foot, what
do astronauts get?**
Missile-toe!

Being cool, brave and good-looking can be tough. It's lonely at the top.

What did the AstroTurf say to the football field?
'Don't move! I gotcha covered!'

'**Knock, knock.**'
'Who's there?'
'**Handsome.**'
'Handsome who?'
'**Hand some of that pizza to me!**'

Velma: **Hey, Fred, why are you folding your tenners in half?**
Fred: **I want to double my money!**

How many Freds would it take to change a lightbulb?
None. Fred's so brave he doesn't mind the dark.

I think it's fair to say that I, Velma, am the true brains behind Mystery, Inc. although I don't like to show off!

What kind of maths has to do with gardening?
Gee-I'm-a-Tree.

What's the best tool to bring to Maths class?
Multi-pliers.

How many feet are in a yard?
Depends on how many people are standing in it!

I'd like to state, for the record, that it's scientifically impossible for us to be totally **HOT** and totally **COOL** at the same time – no matter what Fred says.

What was Daphne's favourite subject in school?
Buy-ology!

Why shouldn't you do maths around cannibals?
Because if you add 4 and 4, you get 8.

What did Shaggy's teachers used to yell at him for NOT doing?
His homework!

Which classes didn't Fred fail?
The ones he didn't take!

All I know is that I'm Daphne – I may not always have the answers, but I know what looks good with any outfit!

What do you call a really groovy beaded watchband?
Accessory to the time.

Why did the vampire fall in love with Daphne?
He said she reminded him of the girl necks door.

Girls just want to have fun . . . and solve the hardest mysteries, and look good while they're doing it.

What did Daphne name her fierce, fire-eating kitty?
Fluffy the Campfire Slayer!

What magazine do monsters read?
Shout!

Why was Daphne looking for the monster snails?
She wanted to give them a manicure.

He's Scooby.

Re's Raggy.

He's usually hungry.

Re's usually rared!

Where do ace detectives like us get our groceries?
The snooper-market.

How did we finally conquer the Giant Hamburger Monster?
We grilled the suspect!

'Knock, knock.'
'Who's there?'
'Men.'
'Men who?'
'No, thanks. Just give me the fries!'

Bravery is overrated!

What did Shaggy yell when he hid beneath his covers?
'I'm not scared, I'm just going undercover!'

What does Scooby like to drink when he's washing down a Scooby Snack?
Dr Pupper.

What looks exactly like Shaggy, but weighs nothing?
His shadow!

What's the difference between Scooby and a painter?
Scooby sheds his coat. A painter coats his shed.

Zoinks!

Scientific Name
Goodus vs Badus

Common Name
**Good Jokes About
Bad Monsters**

**What did the witch
doctor say to Daphne?**
'Voodoo like to
dance?'

**Who does a mummy
take on a date?**
Anyone he can
dig up.

What's a vampire's favourite tree?
A ceme-tree.

12

Shaggy: **I'm a tepee! I'm a wigwam! I'm a tepee! I'm a wigwam!**

Velma: **Relax! You're two tents!**

Shaggy: **Like, I can't help it! We're surrounded by bad guys!**

What's the best way to keep the 10,000 Volt Ghost from striking?
Pay him a good salary!

What's Scooby's idea of the best way to talk to a monster?
From a long, long way away!

What did the monster's mother say when her daughter got older?
'She's certainly gruesome!'

Bestselling Bad-Guy Books

The Mummy's Handbook by I. B. N. Rapt

My Life as a Vampire by Drew Blood

The Werewolf's Confession by Rip U. Tashreds

A Monster's Job by Bea Vishus

Nothing like a good book by a writer who knows the subject!

Bestselling Good-Guy Books

Why I Became a Private Eye by **Wanda Findum**

The Endless Search for Evil by **Sarah Vilinere**

How to Catch a Bad Guy by **Kip Luhkin**

True Tales of Terror by **Dun Chasingools**

Daphne: **Did you hear about the monster who ate a whole family?**
Velma: **That's a little tough to swallow.**

How do you handle a blue monster?
Tell him a joke to cheer him up!

What do you call one hundred acres filled with monsters?
A terror-tory.

What did the vampire do when his shift at work was half over?
He took a coffin break.

What's the Ghost of Redbeard's favourite meal?
Fish and ships.

How much does Redbeard's Ghost pay to have his ears pierced?
A buck-an-ear!

How did the bad guy keep Scooby from barking?
He gave him Hush Puppies.

When did the detective find out the villain was in the belfry?
When the bell tolled.

**What did the ghost of Farmer Brown call his cows
with only two legs?**
Lean beef.

**What did the ghost of Farmer Brown call his cows
with no legs?**
Ground beef.

You can say that again!

Why did the Spirit of the Black Knight stop asking Daphne out on dates?
He knew he didn't stand a ghost of a chance.

Scientific Name
Monstertorium

Common Name
**Creepy Creature
Crack-Ups**

One cannibal asked another cannibal how long people
should be cooked. What did the
second cannibal say?
'Same as short ones.'

Like, don't make jokes
about things that go
bump in the night.
They might hear you!

How did the cannibal
congratulate his friend?
He toasted him.

What did the cannibal say
to her son when he chased
the postman?
'Stop playing with your food.'

Did you hear about the cannibal lion?
He had to swallow his pride!

Where do slimy, oozing, one-eyed monsters shop?
The gross-ery store.

What's the best way to keep a stinky monster from smelling?
Plug his nose!

What did the Giant Slug Monster shout when its victim escaped?
'I'll get you next slime!'

What did one zombie say to another?
'Get a life!'

Why did the Cyclops have to shut down his school?
Because he only had one pupil.

What did the monster couple like to do after dinner?
Go out for an evening troll.

Where do baby ghouls go during the day?
Day scare.

What do you call two witches who live together?
Broom-mates.

Daphne: **What kind of horse should you ride at night?**
Scooby: **Reats me!**
Daphne: **'A night-mare!**

Why did the one-handed monster cross the road?
To get to the secondhand shop.

What did the werewolf say when he left his victim?
'Nice gnawin' you.'

What does Scooby call a deserted town full of great food?
A roast town.

Why did Shaggy confuse a mummy and the packages under his Christmas tree?
One was a wrapped presence and the others were wrapped presents!

Why was Scooby afraid to go to the shoe store?
He was afraid of all the soles!

Why couldn't Scooby and Shaggy find their way out of the ghost town?
They kept coming to dead ends.

Daphne: **Yikes! Frog Man has been here!**
Fred: **How do you know?**
Daphne: **There's an empty Croaka-Cola bottle!**

What do you call a little girl ghoul who climbs trees and runs wild?
A tomb-boy.

What did the zombie say when he buried the detective?
'You're in deep trouble now!'

Why did the skeleton cross the road?
To get to the body shop.

What do skeletons say before they eat?
'Bone appétit!'

Why wouldn't the skeleton cross the road?
He had no guts!

Why didn't the skeleton go to the party?
He had no body to go with.

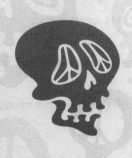

I've got a bone to pick with whoever's making up these jokes!

What did one skeleton say to another when they met on the street?
'Bone-jour'.

What did the extraterrestrial skeleton want to do?
Bone home.

What do you call a skeleton who can't carry a tune?
Bone-deaf.

Scientific Name
Villainous Stupidiferous

Common Name
Big Bad Buffoons!

Why did the monster get arrested for eating his bran flakes?
They thought he was a cereal killer.

Why did the pitcher wear a face mask when his team played the witches?
He heard their bats really flew!

Why wouldn't the vampire eat an orange?
He preferred neck-tarines.

What happened to the nitwit who didn't pay the exorcist?
He was repossessed.

Rupid ris ras rupid roes!

Why did Big Bad Bald Bill paint rabbits on his head?
From a distance, they looked like hares.

Why did the numbskull ghost stay out of the wildlife reserve?
He heard he needed a haunting licence.

Why did Dracula go to New York City?
He wanted to visit the Vampire State Building.

Why did the vampire go to the doctor?
He said his coffin put him flat on his back!

Why did the Headless Horseman open a savings account?
He wanted to get a head.

Why did the mummy refuse to go on vacation?
He didn't want to unwind.

Why did the stupid vampire take the top off his coffin?
He was tired of things going over his head.

Velma: **Did you hear about the ship that was so loaded down with vampires that it sank?**
Shaggy: **Now that's what I call a blood vessel!**

Why did the goblin's wife stop ordering dessert?
She was trying to keep her ghoulish figure.

Why did the mummy avoid a life of crime?
He was afraid of being strip-searched!

'**Knock, knock.**'
'Who's there?'
'**Juan.**'
'Juan who?'
'**Juan monster!**'

'**Knock, knock.**'
'Who's there?'
'**Moira.**'
'Moira who?'
'**Moira monsters!**'

'**Knock, knock.**'
'Who's there?'
'**Ann.**'
'Ann who?'
'**Ann-other monster!**'

'Knock, knock.'
'Who's there?'
'Evan.'
'Evan who?'
'Evan MORE monsters!'

'Knock, knock.'
'Who's there?'
'Howie.'
'Howie who?'
'Howie gonna get away from all these monsters?'

Shaggy: 'Knock, knock.'
Scooby: 'Rho's rhere?'
Shaggy: 'A troll. He's too short to ring the doorbell.'

Nurse: **'Doctor, there's a ghost here to meet you.'**
Doctor: **'Tell her I can't see her.'**

What do you call a really stupid monster who makes nice sweaters?
A knit-wit.

Why couldn't the Ghost of Redbeard play cards while pirates were on his ship?
Because they were standing on the deck.

Ruh-roh! More rupid rokes!

Why did the Abominable Snowman paint his toenails red?
So he could hide in the strawberry patch.

What's white, has a wand and gives money to young vampires?
The Fang Fairy.

Why did the werewolf take so many baths?
He wanted to be a wash-and-werewolf.

Scientific Name
Screaminous Meaminous

Common Name
Yikes 'n' Yuks!

Which monster can you only find in the forest?
Franken-pine.

Which monster can you only find in a cave?
Franken-mine.

Which monster is always at a restaurant?
Franken-dine.

Which monster loves to garden?
Franken-vine.

Like, this is one creepy museum!

What's the cannibal monster's favourite game?
Swallow the Leader!

What do ghosts do to keep safe when they're driving?
They BOO-kle their safety belts.

What does the Abominable Snowman drink after he tramples a village?
Squash.

Where do mummies like to go on holiday?
The Dead Sea.

Where do goblins go to buy stamps?
The ghost office.

What do little girl monsters sell door-to-door?
Ghoul Scout Cookies.

What did Dr Frankenstein say as he put the finishing touches on his new monster creation?
'Let's bolt!'

Velma: **What could possibly be scarier than being asked out on a date?**
Daphne: **Not being asked?**

Which ghoul won the title of Miss Skeleton?
No body.

How does a witch keep her hair looking just right?
Scare-spray.

Which monster is always complaining?
Franken-whine.

Which monster gave up telling bad jokes?
Franken-resign.

What does a ghost read in the morning?
The boos-paper.

What are the two things a cannibal can't eat for breakfast?
Lunch and dinner.

How do you keep a giant monster from charging?
Take away its credit cards.

Fred: **What should you do if you find a bloodthirsty monster in your bed?**

Velma: **Sleep somewhere else.**

How did the newspapers describe the winner of the Miss Monster beauty contest?

'Pretty Ugly!'

What's the worst day of the week to meet a cannibal?

Chews-day.

Why did the cannibal lose his job?
He was buttering up the boss.

What happened to the actors who tried to perform in the haunted theatre?
They got a bad case of stage fright.

What did the phantom e-mail his phantom friend after he'd moved out of town?
'You are mist.'

Shaggy: **Imagine you're trapped in a haunted house filled with vampires and cannibals. How do you survive?**
Velma: **Stop imagining.**

How do vampires celebrate their blessings?
Fangs-giving.

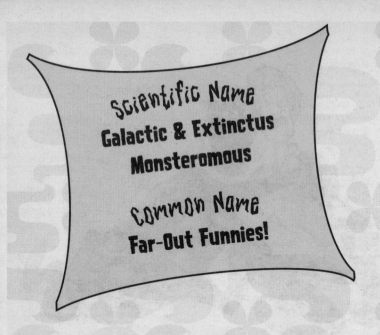

Scientific Name
Galactic & Extinctus Monsteromous

Common Name
Far-Out Funnies!

What did the fire-breathing alien say just before he attacked?
'Nice to heat you!'

Where do aliens leave their spacecrafts?
At parking meteors.

What's an alien's favourite key on the computer?
The space bar.

How do space monsters throw a party?
They planet.

How do space monsters get a baby to fall asleep?
They rocket.

What happened when the fruit-bat monster was put on trial?
He was convicted by a jury of his pears.

What's a big, bad dinosaur monster's favourite number?
Eight

What did Shaggy say after the gang finished fighting the dinosaur's ghost?
'Tyrannosaurus wrecks!'

What's the scariest of the dinosaur monsters?
The terror-dactyl!

How did Velma feel after she was attacked by the prehistoric monster?
Dino-SORE!

Talk about old jokes!

Why did the factory workers run when the vegetarian dinosaur headed towards their building?
Because everyone knows that vegetarians are PLANT eaters!

What kind of spell did the wizard put on the dinosaur?
A Tyrannosaurus hex.

What did the mother buffalo monster say to her son when he left for school?
'Bison!'

How do monsters predict their futures?
They read their horror-scopes.

Why do skeletons stay so calm?
Nothing gets under their skin.

How do monsters like their eggs?
Terror-fried.

Fred: **Why did the ghost wear sunglasses?**
Daphne: **I don't know. Why?**
Fred: **He thought they made him look ghoul.**

**What do you call a vampire who
falls for practical jokes?**
A real sucker!

What did Velma say to the ancient, smelly swamp monster?
'You extinct!'

What kind of music did the mummy like best?
Ragtime!

What did the cannibal order at the fast-food restaurant?
A hand-burger.

What do you call a skeleton that refuses to work?
Lazybones!

Where did the phantom go to pick up his mail?
The dead letter office.

Why are ghost gatherings so boring?
There's no one to be the life of the party!

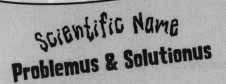

**What does Scooby do when he
needs help contacting monsters?**
He calls in the fur-ensic experts!

**Why was Dr Frankenstein
depressed?**
He'd just broken up with his
ghoul-friend.

**How did the mad scientist invent
mosquito repellent?**
From scratch.

Daphne: Knock, knock.
Fred: Who's there?
Daphne: Police.
Fred: Police who?
Daphne: Police stop these terrible jokes!

How does Velma's favourite bedtime story begin?
Once upon a crime . . .

What did the detective say when his boss asked him about the search for the Giant Insect Monster?
'I'm looking for the ant-sir!'

What do you get when you cross a great detective with a ghost?
Sherlock Moans.

What do you get when you cross a great detective with a skeleton?
Sherlock Bones.

What do you get when you cross a great detective with a bad comedian?
Sherlock Groans.

What do you get when you cross a great detective with a banker?
Sherlock Loans.

What do you get when you cross a great detective with an ice cream truck?
Sherlock Cones.

What did E.T. say when he needed a detective to find his missing spaceship?
Phone Holmes.

These jokes are a crime!

How did Count Dracula write his life story?
In blood type.

How did Dracula describe his date with the pretty robot?
'Love at first byte!'

Why did Dracula punish his son?
He was acting like a spoiled bat.

What does Dracula drink to wake up?
Coffin-ated beverages.

Shaggy: **What do little vampire detectives learn in kindergarten?**
Scooby: **Ri ron't rhow. Rhat?**
Shaggy: **The alpha-bat!**

How did the mad scientist transform the train conductor into a monster cannibal?
He hypnotized him, and then told him to listen to his train – choo-choo-choo.

Why did the monster have a bath after eating all his victims?
He wanted to make a clean getaway.

What was Velma's favourite game when she was little?
Corpse and robbers.

What did the detective tell his neighbours when he left town in search of a witch?
'I'm going away for a spell.'

Jinkies! That's spooky!

What book was written by a guy who was attacked by a werewolf?
How to Survive a Monster Attack by I. M. Fien

Why do detectives have such a hard time catching ghosts?
It's difficult to pin anything on them.

Scientific Name
Coolsville Superstarus

Common Name
Hollywood Hysteria!

What did the star of the blockbuster vampire movie do when he became a big star?
He started a fang club.

What did one Hollywood witch say to another?
'Let's make movie magic!'

Where does the skeleton starlet spend her days off?
In bed eating bonebones.

Making a movie is not all fun and games . . . a lot of it is hair and make-up!

Why are there so many movie-star werewolves?
They like living in Howlywood.

What kind of ice cream did the movie-star vampire have in his dressing room?
Vein-illa.

How did the mad scientist become such a famous comedian?
He had a way of leaving people in stitches.

Why did the skeleton think he was going to get the starring role in the monster movie?
He could feel it in his bones.

What did the director of *The Monster Lumberjack* have to learn NOT to say while they were shooting the movie?
'Ax-tion!' And, CUT!'

Where did the mummy actor like to stand when he was on stage?
Dead centre.

Why did the mummy get hired to stand in for the movie star?
He was a dead ringer.

How did the director address his monster star?
Very politely.

What movie was Count Dracula the star of?
The Vampire Strikes Back.

Which movie starred a bunch of monster dolls?
Toy Gory.

What movie's superhero got run over by a wild bunch of giant monsters?
Flat-man.

What is the greatest movie ever made?
Scooby-Doo 2, of course!

Show business is my laugh – I mean, life!

Just remember

– when it comes to defending yourself against monsters,
there's nothing scarier than a bad joke.